To:

Mal...

From:

The Grateful Greggs

Date:

27 March
2020

A faithful and true friend is a living treasure.

Robert Hall

Some friendships are
made by nature, some
by contract, some by interest,
and some by souls.

Jeremy Taylor

Friends Forever, Facing Whatever

Artwork by Lori Siebert

HARVEST HOUSE PUBLISHERS

EUGENE, OREGON

Friends Forever, Facing Whatever

Artwork copyright © Lori Siebert

Published by Harvest House Publishers
Eugene, Oregon 97402
www.harvesthousepublishers.com

ISBN 978-0-7369-4510-3

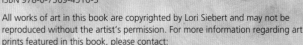

Courtney Davis, Inc.
340 Main Street
Franklin, Tennessee 37064

Design and production by Mary pat Design, Westport, Connecticut

Harvest House Publishers has made every effort to trace the ownership of all poems and quotes. In the event of a question arising from the use of a poem or quote, we regret any error made and will be pleased to make the necessary correction in future editions of this book.

All Scripture quotations are taken from The Holy Bible, *New International Version*® *NIV*®. Copyright © 1973, 1978, 1984, 2011 by Biblica, Inc.™ Used by permission. All rights reserved worldwide.

Printed in China

18 19 20 / LP / 10 9 8 7 6 5 4

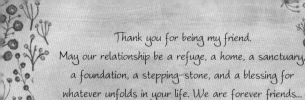

Thank you for being my friend.
May our relationship be a refuge, a home, a sanctuary,
a foundation, a stepping-stone, and a blessing for
whatever unfolds in your life. We are forever friends...

Many kinds of fruit grow upon the tree of Life,
but none so sweet as friendship. Lucy Larcom

There is nothing like putting the
shine on another's face to put
the shine on our own.

William Channing Gannett

Through Laughter

You, my friend, teach me to lighten up! When I witness your easy laugh and your unwavering belief in goodness, I am inspired to embrace the silly and delightful moments that fill a lifetime. Thank you for giving me permission and encouragement to let the little things go so that there is more room for joy, great conversation, and generosity.

Friends are the sunshine of life.

John Hay

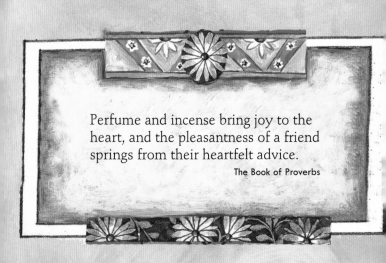

Perfume and incense bring joy to the heart, and the pleasantness of a friend springs from their heartfelt advice.

The Book of Proverbs

While I keep my senses
I shall prefer nothing to a pleasant friend.

Horace

The greatest happiness in life is
the conviction that we are loved,
loved for ourselves, or rather
loved in spite of ourselves.

Victor Hugo

It is a friendly heart that has plenty of friends.

William Thackeray

Of all the things which wisdom provides
to make life entirely happy, much the
greatest is the possession of friendship.

Epicurus

My friend peers in on me with merry
Wise face, and though the sky stay dim,
The very light of day, the very
Sun's self comes in with him. A.C. Swinburne

The mind never unbends itself so agreeably as in the conversation of a well-chosen friend. There is indeed no blessing of life that is any way comparable to the enjoyment of a discreet and virtuous friend. It eases and unloads the mind, clears and improves the understanding, engenders thoughts and knowledge, animates virtue and good resolutions, soothes and allays the passions, and finds employment for most of the vacant hours of life.

Joseph Addison

11

Love is flower-like;
Friendship is like a sheltering tree.

S.T. Coleridge

Through Tears

We know how to shower each other with grace when the tears of sadness or frustration fall. Whether we are dabbing our eyes during a sappy, romantic movie or sobbing about a great loss, there is never a need to explain. You offer just the right words at the right time. And when words won't do, you offer your shoulder to lean on. The comfort of friendship in the midst of sorrows, big and small, is a lasting treasure.

A beloved
friend does not
fill one part of
the soul, but,
penetrating the
whole, becomes
connected with
all feeling.
William Ellery Channing

14

The man that
comforts a
desponding friend
with words alone,
does nothing.

He's a friend
indeed, who
proves himself a
friend in need.

Plautus

Friendship throws a greater lustre on prosperity, while it lightens adversity by sharing in its griefs and anxieties.

Cicero

There is no better medicine for grief than the advice of a good and honored friend. He who, in his sufferings, excites and tries to soothe his mind by wine, though he may have pleasure for a moment, has a double portion of pain afterwards.

Euripides

Said a wise man to one in deep sorrow, "I did not come to comfort you; God only can do that; but I did come to say how deeply and tenderly I feel for you in your affliction."

Tryon Edwards

Small service is true service while it lasts,
Of humblest friends, bright creature, scorn not one;
The daisy by the shadow that it casts
Protects the lingering dewdrop from the sun.

William Wordsworth

Friendship is
steady and
peaceful. . .
it doubles our
joys, divides
our griefs, and
warms our lives
with a steady
flame.

Charles Reade

19

Hand grasps hand, eye lights eye, in good
Friendship. And great hearts expand and
grow one in the sense of this world's life.

Robert Browning

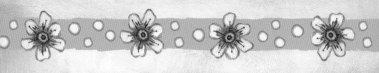

Through This Moment

Oh friend, I love how we help each other be fully present in our lives. When I want to rush by a life lesson, you remind me to pay attention. When you pass a cozy café on the way to a grander destination, I remind you to savor the ambience of a local spot. Every moment I spend as your friend has meaning and joy.

The conversation of a friend brightens the eyes.

Persian Proverb

21

A little peaceful home
bounds all my wants
and wishes; add to
this my book and
friend—and this is
happiness supreme.

Michel de Montaigne

22

Friendship is a union of spirits,
a marriage of hearts, and
the bond thereof virtue.

William Penn

Of all the best things upon earth,

I hold that a faithful friend

is the best.

Owen Meredith

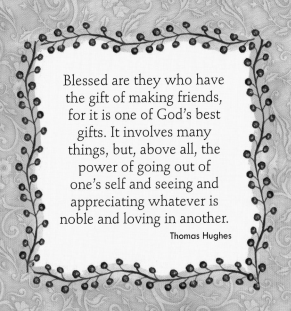

Blessed are they who have the gift of making friends, for it is one of God's best gifts. It involves many things, but, above all, the power of going out of one's self and seeing and appreciating whatever is noble and loving in another.

Thomas Hughes

He has the substance of all bliss
To whom a virtuous friend is given:
So sweet harmonious friendship is,
Add but eternity, you'll make it heaven.

John Norris

The expensiveness of friendship does not lie in
what one does for one's friends, but in what,
out of regard for them, one leaves undone.

Henrik Ibsen

26

A true friend is forever a friend.

George MacDonald

God never loved me in so sweet a way before;
'Tis He alone who can such blessings send;
And when His love would new expression find
He brought thee to me and He said,
    "Behold a friend."

Gladys Sylvester Olds

Through the Years

Since the day our friendship formed,
I have been blessed. Neither great distance nor
time apart comes between kindred spirits. We
always know that the one is praying for and
thinking of the other. I'm grateful that we get
to share our future years with the gift of such
a connection. It's almost worth getting old for!

My treasures are my friends.

Constantius

There is no friend like an old friend
who has shared our morning days,
no greeting like his welcome, no
homage like his praise.

Oliver Wendell Holmes

Change, Care, nor Time while life endure
Shall spoil our ancient friendship sure.

Andrew Lang

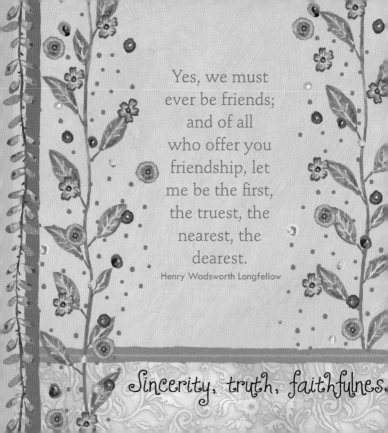

Yes, we must ever be friends; and of all who offer you friendship, let me be the first, the truest, the nearest, the dearest.

Henry Wadsworth Longfellow

Sincerity, truth, faithfulnes

Friendship does not spring up and
grow great and become perfect
all at once, but requires time and
the nourishment of thoughts.

Dante

...me into the very essence of friendship.

William Ellery Channing

Time draweth wrinkles in a
fair face, but addeth fresh
colors to a fast friend.

John Lyle

A day for toil, an hour for sport,
But for a friend life is too short.

Ralph Waldo Emerson

In friendship we find nothing false or insincere; everything is straightforward, and springs from the heart.

Cicero

What is a friend?
I will tell you.
It is a person with whom
you dare to be yourself.

Frank Crane

Through Adventures

Whether we are trying on shoes or flying across the country, we make our time together an adventure. We know how to live out the sweet life! We savor late night conversations, road trips without destinations, cold glasses of fresh lemonade, and the discovery of great books. Most of all, we enjoy and value the delicious gift of friendship.

Friendship heightens all our affections. We receive all the ardor of our friend in addition to our own. The communication of minds gives to each the fervor of each.

William Ellery Channing

I could not live without the love of my friends.

John Keats

It is a good and safe rule to sojourn in many places, as if you meant to spend your life there, never omitting an opportunity of doing a kindness or speaking a true word or making a friend.

John Ruskin

The happiest life is that which constantly exercises and educates what is best in us.

Philip Hamerton

39

It is a good thing to be rich,
and a good thing to be strong,
but it is a better thing to be
beloved of many friends.

Euripides

A faithful friend is
better than gold—a
medicine for misery,
an only possession.

Robert Burton

Life should be
fortified by many
friendships.
To love and
to be loved is
the greatest
happiness of
existence.

Sydney Smith

Words cannot express the joy which a friend imparts;
they only can know who have experienced. A friend
is dearer than the light of heaven, for it would be
better for us that the sun were extinguished than
that we should be without friends.

Saint John Chrysostom

I have sped by land and sea, and mingled with much people,
But never yet could find a spot unsunned by human kindness;
Some more, and some less; but, truly, all can claim a little:
And a man may travel through the world, and sow it thick with friendships.

Martin Farquhar Tupper

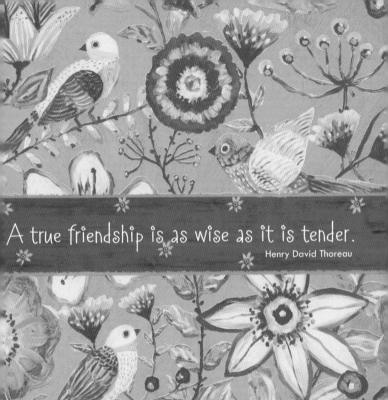

A true friendship is as wise as it is tender.

Henry David Thoreau

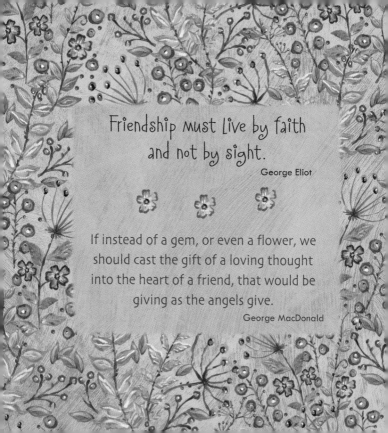

Friendship must live by faith
and not by sight.

George Eliot

If instead of a gem, or even a flower, we
should cast the gift of a loving thought
into the heart of a friend, that would be
giving as the angels give.

George MacDonald

Through Fears

You and I, we inch up to the edge of
our comfort zones. We contemplate leaps of
faith. When worries fill our minds, the steady
flow of encouraging words between friends
buoys us with hope and promise. Together, we
can face whatever comes our way because
we know the strength of a forever friend's
faith, support, and presence. I'm so thankful
for your compassion and courage.

Heaven forming each on other to depend,
A master, or a servant, or a friend,
Bids each on other for assistance call,
Till one man's weakness grows the strength of all.

Alexander Pope

God wills that we have sorrows here,
And we will share it;
Whisper thy sorrow in my ear,
That I may also bear it.
If anywhere our trouble seems
To find an end,
'Tis in the fairy land of dreams,
Or with a friend.

Lord Alfred Tennyson

A friend is worth all the hazards we can run.

Edward Young

Friendship, a dear balm
Whose coming is as light and music are
'Mid dissonance and gloom a star
Which moves not 'mid the moving heavens alone;
A smile among dark frowns: a beloved light:
A solitude, a refuge, a delight.

Percy Bysshe Shelley

Friendship is the greatest bond in the world. Jeremy Taylor

Life is made up, not of great sacrifices or duties, but of little things, in which smiles and kindness, and small obligations given habitually, are what preserve the heart and secure comfort.

Sir Humphry Davy

One of the
most beautiful
qualities of true
friendship is to
understand and to
be understood.

Lucius Seneca

Through Changes

The foundation of our friendship helps us weather the storms and reach new heights. We get to dance on the common ground of ideas and joys. And in the space between our differences is a bridge of perspective and wisdom. We have learned to overcome life's trials and to come alongside one another with compassion. Circumstances surely change, but our friendship is forever.

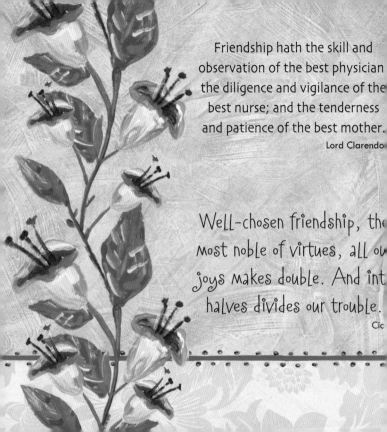

Friendship hath the skill and observation of the best physician the diligence and vigilance of the best nurse; and the tenderness and patience of the best mother.

Lord Clarendo

Well-chosen friendship, the most noble of virtues, all ou joys makes double. And int halves divides our trouble.

Cic

I cannot contentedly frame a prayer for myself in particular, without a catalogue for my friends; nor request a happiness, wherein my sociable disposition doth not desire the fellowship of my neighbor.

Thomas Browne

Amid the tireless breaking of the billows on the shores of experience, there is no surer anchorage than a friendship that "beareth all things, believeth all things, hopeth all things."

Sarah B. Cooper

Of all the heavenly gifts that mortal men commend, What trusty treasure in the world can countervail a friend?

Nicholas Grimald

But if the while I think on thee, dear friend, all losses are restored and sorrows end.

54

William Shakespeare

After a certain age a
new friend is a wonder.
There is the age of blossoms
and sweet budding green,
the age of generous summer,
the autumn when the leaves
drop, and then winter
shivering and bare.

William Thackeray

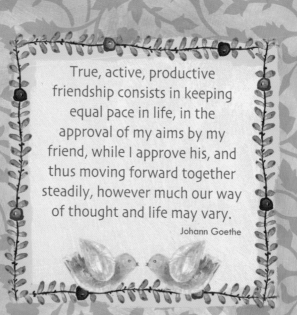

True, active, productive friendship consists in keeping equal pace in life, in the approval of my aims by my friend, while I approve his, and thus moving forward together steadily, however much our way of thought and life may vary.

Johann Goethe

Such is friendship,
that through it
we love places and
seasons; for as bright
bodies emit rays
at a distance, and
flowers drop their
sweet leaves on the
ground around them,
so friends impart favor
even to the places
where they dwell.

Saint John Chrysostom

The love of friendship is the most perfect form of loving.

Cardinal Manning

Through Cheers

Hooray for you, my friend! We have rejoiced in many wonderful happenings together, but the longest lasting celebration is the 24/7 party of gratitude that goes on in my heart. I'm so thankful for the many ways you share your kindness and hopefulness with those in your life. Three cheers for my forever friend.

Friendship is the
holiest of gifts,
God can bestow nothing
more sacred upon us!
It enhances every joy,
mitigates every pain.
Everyone can have a friend
Who himself knows how
to be a friend.

Teidge

What can be more delightful than to have one to whom you can speak on all subjects just as to yourself? Where would be the great enjoyment in prosperity if you had not one to rejoice in it equally with yourself? And adversity would indeed be difficult to endure without someone who would bear it even with greater regret than yourself.

Cicero

To love and be loved is the greatest happiness of existence.

Sydney Smith

I want a warm and faithful friend,
To cheer the adverse hour;
Who ne'er to flatter will descend,
Nor bend the knee to power.
A friend to chide me when I'm wrong,
My inmost soul to see;
And that my friendship prove as strong
To him as his to me.

John Quincy Adams

The making of friends, who are real friends, is the best token we have of a man's success in life.

Edward Everett Hale

As I love
nature, as I
love singing
birds, and
gleaming
stubble, and
flowing rivers,
and morning,
and evening,
and summer,
and winter,
I love thee,
My friend.

Henry David Thoreau

63

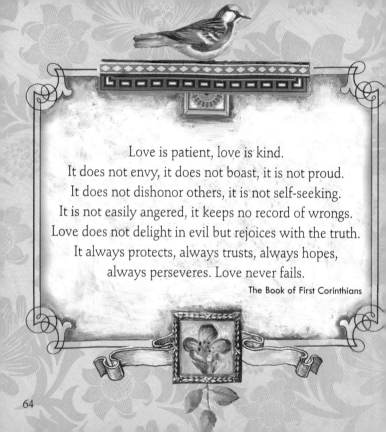

Love is patient, love is kind.
It does not envy, it does not boast, it is not proud.
It does not dishonor others, it is not self-seeking.
It is not easily angered, it keeps no record of wrongs.
Love does not delight in evil but rejoices with the truth.
It always protects, always trusts, always hopes,
always perseveres. Love never fails.

The Book of First Corinthians